I0488687

This book was published in New York City in February 2015 by Tony Bacigalupo.

It was updated for print in June 2018.

It was edited by Amy Segreti, but please don't fault her for any errors you find here because I broke the golden rule and edited the book after she completed her work!

Set in Museo.

The cover icons all come from the Noun Project, which is really amazing. Check it out. Mug icon #74735 is by Rohith M S. #27500 is by Mark Caron. #12288 is by Killian McIlroy. #48905 is by Wilson Joseph.

No more sink full of mugs.

Before we begin, this is super important:

Make sure you're registered so you can access updates and included resources!

By purchasing this book, you've also granted yourself access to really handy supplemental resources that complement what you'll be reading here. The trick is, if you bought this through a platform like Amazon, I may not be able to reach you to get you access to these things.

Let's fix that right now! Head to nwc.co/mugs-book and pop your name and email into the super simple form there.

Thanks!
Tony

Table of contents

Sinks full of mugs are awful.

Just think about them. Don't think for too long; doing so might ruin your day. A sink full of mugs just... stinks.

There is only one thing worse than a sink full of mugs, and that's a leaky trash bag. But let's not go there; I've literally had nightmares about that one and maybe you have too.

Okay, the other thing that's worse than a sink full of mugs is the knowledge that once you're done loading each and every one of them into the dishwasher, the sink will be full again before you know it.

You might feel compelled to send out another angry email out to your members, reminding them that the rules clearly state they must put their used mugs in the dishwasher. You feel awful, because you hate being mean to the people who pay your bills, but to make matters worse you don't expect what you're telling them to have much of an effect.

How did it get this way? What's happening here?

Sinks full of mugs are symbolic of something.

They signify a culture of "someone else will deal with this." They're evidence that there are people among us who think they're too busy to do their part, or that someone else should pick up after them.

That doesn't mean these people are evil or even malicious in their intent. They're probably just busy. Let's face it—we've left our fair share of mugs in sinks too, right? If it's happening in your shared space, however, it may be a sign that you've got some work to do.

If this is your reality, let's talk about how we can stop this from happening and start steering things in a healthier direction.

Building and maintaining a healthy culture in a shared space is an elusive task. For things to work, you can work feverishly to maintain order yourself, but you might already know that this strategy isn't sustainable. Putting it all on yourself will inevitably lead to resentment and burnout.

To mange this well, you're going to need some help from your fellow community members. But how do you get these people, who are likely paying customers, to be on board with helping you make your job easier? That seems a little greedy, doesn't it?

Creating circumstances that invite and empower people to coexist in a healthy way with each other is the only way I know of to achieve a truly healthy workplace culture.

Getting there isn't easy or obvious, but it doesn't have to be crazy hard. In many cases, there are simple ways to approach common challenges that can go far in fostering exactly the kind of culture you dream of having.

This book exists to help you avoid the nightmare and cultivate a better culture in your workspace. It draws on our more than seven years of experience developing and managing shared workspaces, in particular at New Work City, a coworking space I helped build and run.

A great workspace is one where the sink never gets a chance to fill up. This book is here to help with not just your sink, but also the small and large things that can shift an entire culture for the better. Thanks for buying it.

Ready to steer your culture in the right direction? Read on!

Why this book?

It struck me while I was having tea with my friend and fellow New Work City coworker David Haddad at a loud Williamsburg bar one night. David was talking about his experiences at our space and how it contrasted with his experience at other coworking spaces. He mentioned that one of the things that worked in our space was how we had simple systems in place that made potentially difficult things easier. In many cases, these simple systems fostered a sense of trust and created space for healthier culture.

I can't tell you that what we did is the only or best way to do something. You have to decide what works best for you. What I can do is tell you what we've done and what we've learned. If we've found some success with something, then perhaps learning from our experience can better inform your own.

When you run a workspace, it can be really hard to solve a lot of common problems in ways that preserve and extend a healthy culture. To suffer the fate of someone running a workspace that's mired in strict rules and resentful members is not something I would wish on anyone, so if this book helps in any way to rescue you from that fate, then I'll be grateful for having written it.

in strict rules and resentful members is not something I would wish on anyone, so if this book helps in any way to rescue you from that fate, then I'll be grateful for having written it.

Before we begin

This is a small book. I purposely made this book small, with a number of things in mind:

- **I've tried writing longer books.** Have you read them? Neither have I. That's because they don't exist. I wanted to write something limited enough in scope that I'd have a better chance of actually shipping it. (And look! It worked!)

- **I hate reading books packed with fluff.** Don't you? I can't stand when I read page after page of stuff that doesn't seem to have much substance. I wonder whether the author had to stretch their material to hit a minimum page count, not unlike something you might see in a high school term paper.

- **I feel like I can give you far more than your money's worth** without having to prove myself with a lot of theory and research. The things we'll cover in this book have been extremely valuable to my community; I hope they're valuable to yours too. If you read this all the way through and don't feel it was worth your while, let me know and we'll sort it out, okay?

- **You're busy.** If you're reading this book, then you probably have a lot to tend to. Let's cut to the chase, right? I'd be surprised if you even read this entire section.

Backstory

What you read here is largely a result of things I've learned in my experience running New Work City, a coworking space I co-founded in 2008 and ran through 2015. Since this book was published in 2015, everything you read from here onwards is written in the present tense.

Consider this an insight into a time when we were in the midst of things, giving you our insider's download after over seven years of operation.

Much of what you'll read involves techniques I've concocted myself, but in some cases other people were involved. I'll give credit where it's due whenever possible, but if you think I may have missed something, please let me know so I can correct it and take the affected parties out for compensation drinks.

You'll see some other names in this book.

- **Peter Chislett** is my business partner and Deputy Mayor of New Work City, though he maintains that he has never formally taken on a job title. He brings a combination of business experience, consistency, and a level head that I, well, don't. I'm very grateful to have him as a partner.

- **Sarah Feliciano** is our Space Captain. She's essentially the person we pay a full-time salary to manage the place.

- **Veronica Ludwig** was the previous Space Captain, and was responsible for helping us get a lot of our ducks in a row.

- **Leo Newball** is our Minster of Fun, the creator of Snack Wars™, and a really good friend of mine.

- We also have a number of **Space Agents**, who volunteer at the front desk a few times a week in exchange for a free membership. We'll talk more about that later.

You'll see me use the word "we" fairly often throughout this book.

When I use the word "we," I'm deliberately referring to an amorphous group of people that may include any of the folks I've just mentioned, other people I used to work with, and/or other coworkers.

Many of the things that have come out of New Work City arose out of conversations and modifications that involved all kinds of people; in some cases, even I don't know exactly who played what role to which degree. That's part of the beauty of what we've got going.

You can learn more about New Work City by heading to nwc.co/3/backstory.

When we closed our space (which you can read about there: nwc.co/3/we-got-away-with-it), I turned my attention more towards continuing to help many other people build thriving spaces around the world, which I've been doing ever since.

My consultancy for that is called... wait for it... New Work Cities.

Learn more about how this consultancy can help you at nwc.co.

Ready? Let's get rolling!

Handy rules of thumb

If you can only spare a few minutes before your busy life takes your attention elsewhere, give this section a quick skim. These basic principles are behind much of what you'll read in this book and can be applied to any situation.

Over the years, we've discovered or developed a few handy rules of thumb that we come back to again and again to handle an infinite number of unpredictable situations. Propagating these ideas not just among our staff but members themselves helps us head off countless challenges before they even happen.

Before we dive into the specific systems we use, let's look at these high-level approaches so you can have an idea of the approaches we've taken that drive not only the things we've developed already, but help us handle situations not covered in this book. Let's start with those, shall we?

1. Treat people like human beings.

Each human being you encounter on this earth is a living, breathing soul that has wants and hopes and dreams. They want to find love. They cry sometimes. The more you practice awareness of this fact in everything you do, the more likely the people you deal with will reciprocate accordingly. This gives you a powerful starting point for developing a healthy culture.

2. Value relationships over transactions.

You're managing a business. You deal with humans. It's easy to think of things in terms of a cold, untrusting, business-to-customer relationship. This is the opposite of what we want. When someone walks into New Work City for the first time, their guard tends to be up. They brace for a sales pitch. We work to defray those fears immediately. When I talk to a newcomer, I'm quick to emphasize that we don't have investors and don't have a mandate to maximize profits. We're here for each other.

If we did have investors, I'd emphasize that we're in the business of doing good for the people we seek to serve. The point is to alleviate people of the notion that we are simply a business that cares only about making money.

3. Make everything visibly and obviously accessible.

Don't expect people to read your emails or written materials. Put clear, friendly instructions in plain sight where people might discover them at the right moment. This helps to foster an environment that's more self-sufficient.

4. Empower people to handle things themselves wherever possible.

Look for opportunities to reduce load on your staff while making things easier on members who can rest easy knowing they don't have to ask someone else to get what they need.

5. Trust by default.

When you offer your vulnerability to someone and trust them not to violate it, a powerful thing happens in that person: they start to develop a sense of responsibility. This is a critical starting point for a healthy relationship.

6. Remind people to use their conscience.

Hard rules can't account for everything. A lot of things in a shared work environment, and society in general, come down to personal judgment. When someone asks what the rule is for a situation that has no specific rule but does have an implied etiquette, we remind people of the mantra of Pinocchio's sidekick, Jiminy Cricket: "Always let your conscience be your guide."

(This is particularly handy when people ask if it's okay to take phone calls at their desks.)

7. Practice relentless positivity.

This was one of the first principles I learned when I worked at an after-hours educational center for elementary school-age kids. No matter what the situation, we were told to find a positive way to approach it. When you're practicing this, the words you say and the actions you take will always be pointed in a constructive direction, regardless of the circumstances.

It doesn't mean you have to be a pushover. You can stand up for your values and defend your community with a positive attitude in nearly any situation; it often just takes practice and patience.

8. Avoid hard rules.

Have you ever seen a sign posted by an authority figure that says in hardcore caps-lock "NO REFUNDS" / "NO DOGS ALLOWED" / "RENT MUST BE PAID BY THE FIRST OF THE MONTH" / "DON'T EVEN THINK ABOUT PARKING HERE" and so on? How does it make you feel? When I see signs like that, I feel antagonized by someone I haven't even met. I don't feel a ton of sympathy. I certainly don't feel compelled to be on my best behavior.

If, instead, you use signage and other language to inform people about circumstances in a way that respects their autonomy, you might get people to want to behave the way you want them to.

—

To distill it further: Be nice. Be human. Be authentic. Embody the culture you'd like to see reflected back. In doing so, you'll make it a lot easier for the people around you to do the same. I've sometimes been in extremely tight spots with no obvious answers and only got out of them unscathed because I employed at least one if not several of these principles.

12 Simple Systems for Happy, Empowered Communities

The meat and potatoes! Here are 12 simple systems we developed. Let's get to it!

[1] We celebrate when people clear the sink.

Conquering this has been one of our greatest challenges—and greatest successes. After years of struggle, the solution I devised was so deceptively simple that I was shocked at how easy it could be.

The mugs were piling up, and it was getting hard to keep up without building ample doses of resentment. We had to post some kind of signage, but I didn't want it to be negative: "Don't leave your damn mugs in the sink!" When does that ever work? That's not us.

So I thought hard about how we could take a positive approach to a difficult, frustrating situation. After doing a little brainstorming, I designed a sign that said this:

"This is the list of the amazing people who have cleaned out the sink. They have braved the smelly and the slimy for the rest of us. Sink cleaners, we salute you."

Below that was a space for people to put their name and a tally of how many times they'd helped clean out extra dishes from the sink. I printed it, laminated it, and posted it above the sink with a whiteboard marker.

Before long, the list on the sign started to grow, and the number of dishes in the sink started to shrink. Magic!

Benefits

- **People who already help keep the sink clean feel valued.** There are a few superhero members who go the extra mile to help maintain the place. By calling to public attention a celebration of their good deeds, we help ensure they know they're appreciated.

- **People see an opportunity to help.** A lot of time, people are more than happy to help—they just need some direction. Someone who notices the sign as they approach the sink might delight at an opportunity to contribute in a way that requires no more effort than tossing a few items into the dishwasher.

- **People are less likely to leave their mug in the sink.** The Tragedy of the Commons starts the moment after the first mug is left in the sink. From that point onward, every subsequent person who visits will be more likely to leave their mug in the sink too—after all, there's already one mug in the sink, why not two, right?

  From that point onward, every subsequent person who visits will be more likely to leave their mug in the sink too—after all, there's already one mug in the sink, why not two, right?

  An empty sink, however, carries with it a far greater message: *This sink is empty. We all work to keep it that way. Are you sure you're too busy to deal with your mug right now?*

We've found that, by rewarding people for helping to clean out the sink, it ends up being empty more often, and less people leave their mugs in the sink in the first place.

It's a simple thing. It doesn't always work perfectly, but it's positive, it's fun, it sends a message about how we do things here, and it certainly doesn't hurt to try.

Homework: Make a sheet that invites people to publicly proclaim their helpfulness and celebrate it.

Use the included template, or don't! Make it simple and friendly. If you have a laminating machine (and I recommend that you do), laminate the sign and post it somewhere visible.

Then, most importantly, start using it. Look for opportunities to invite other people to participate as well. Allocating time to just hang out in the kitchen or other common gathering area tends to lead to good things.

[2] We let members be in charge of the coffee.

Coffee is one of our biggest expenses. We go through a lot of it. It's also something that requires a lot of maintenance. Once our thermos is emptied, it must be refilled promptly to stave off revolt. To put the duty of making the coffee every time on the shoulders of a paid employee would add about a half-dozen unexpectedly urgent tasks to their daily queue.

Anyone who manages a shared workspace can tell you that there is no shortage of interruptions to deal with. If there's a way we can cut down the number of these daily distractions, we must.

So we train members in how to run the coffee pot. Of all the members at New Work City, only a portion regularly drink the coffee, and a smaller portion of those people drink it like clockwork. These people are effectively deputies of your municipality's coffee district; they simply need to be empowered.

These members are motivated by their desire to have coffee when they want it. When the coffee runs out, they make more. No need to wait for an employee to get around to it. After years of doing things this way, I'm actually a little afraid to make the coffee for fear that I'll not do it exactly the way that the members have decreed works best for them. Why disturb a system that works?

Homework: Document your coffee-making process.

Lighten your labor load by making it easy for anyone to refill your coffee maker. Next time you make a fresh pot (or urn, as I've learned is the proper term for the large pot we use), document in excruciating detail each step that goes into it. Look for opportunities to label the locations of key supplies and consolidate the relevant materials as close by and as accessible as possible.

When you've got all of your steps ready to go, type them up, print them out, laminate them, and post them up in a highly visible spot right by or above the coffee pot. Make sure to use friendly language that conveys an invitation to help make the space run better.

[3] We give everyone a way to connect with each other though an online discussion group.

We use Google Groups, which is free, simple and easy enough for anyone to use. Aside from our physical space, I consider it to be our best resource for connecting members, because it can instantly match two people to each other without the need for a middleman.

Directing people to the Google Group is a constant mantra. I tell people that by messaging the group, they can make use of the collective mind of the entire membership (and many former members as well, because we don't remove members after they cancel their memberships), which is far more powerful than by talking just to me. I may know some people and some answers, but if you message this group, you're far more likely to reach someone who has the exact answer you need. Countless times over the years, people have connected to each other through the group.

How people use the group

- **They introduce themselves.** If they're new in the space, they might want to simply put themselves out there and let people know they're around and available. Good things often come just from this simple introduction.

- **They post specific questions.** They might be technical or legal in nature, or something specific to the kind of work they're doing. In response, they'll either get the answer they're looking for or a connection to a person who has the answers.

- **They post gigs they're hiring for.** It might be for their own company or for someone they work for. It might be a contract or a full-time gig.

- **They post upcoming events they're going to.** These are often events that are valuable to other members. When members go together to an external event, good things tend to happen for everyone involved.

- **They post about food they brought into the space to share.** This may sound facile, but people love sharing food. They're grateful, and they show it.

The key is that we look for every opportunity to give people permission and encouragement to post to this group. It's easy for people to feel intimidated; I am often asked whether posting a particular thing is worth bothering everyone else about. While we do want to be considerate for people's inboxes, the general attitude among members has been overwhelmingly in support of people erring on the side of sharing more.

Every day, people ask questions and get answers. The value of this should not be underestimated.

[4] We're intentional but not overly pushy about onboarding new members.

Overcoming the perception that we're simply in the business of renting workspace is one of our great challenges. While our business model is predicated on people paying to access a physical space, the real value we're providing—and the reason people come in every day—is for access to a group of people who have developed a valuable culture.

A lot of times, people don't even know that when they sign up. They think what they want is workspace. That's fine, but we know that before long they will likely realize what their real needs are. This is when we have an opportunity to show them the real value of membership in a coworking space.

The challenge lies in making opportunities available to newcomers to plug into that social dynamic in a way that doesn't impose. I dreamed for a long time of a membership in which everyone was highly engaged, highly connected and highly social with everyone else. It took me about five years to realize that this was neither practical nor desirable. In reality, every community should have a diverse population of people who can participate in any of a variety of ways that might suit them years to realize that this was neither practical nor desirable. In reality, every community should have a diverse population of people who can participate in any of a variety of ways that might suit them best. They should also be able to move fluidly between levels and types of participation as their circumstances change.

I should also note that many, if not most, of our members would identify as introverts. Perhaps the same is the case with your community. Introversion, however, is not equivalent to being antisocial. Introverts can be very social, when the circumstances allow for it.

To accommodate the full spectrum of possibility for each person, we create a variety of circumstances that invite people to connect in different ways. We can't predict or dictate exactly which avenue will work for each person, but by making a suite of opportunities available, odds are good that one of them will stick.

Ways members can connect to each other:

- **They feel free to talk to each other in the space.** It may seem obvious, but often people need to be explicitly told that it's okay to speak to your neighbor. We remind people to be considerate and not bother people who are obviously busy, but oftentimes a good connection is just a simple hello away.

- **They spend some time in the kitchen.** This area in particular is great, because it's a place where people are away from their computer screens and potentially taking a break from work. The kitchen is perhaps our most important social space.

  (A handy aside: If you're ever feeling disconnected from your membership, get to work early and hang out in the kitchen area for an hour or two as people arrive for the day. Talk to people about anything, but in particular anything that isn't related to business. Magic happens for me every time I do this.)

- **They can use our online discussion group.** This is especially handy for members who don't come in often, or who might not be as comfortable meeting strangers face-to-face.

- **They can attend a Welcome Aboard Member Meeting.** This is our monthly gathering that gives everyone a low-barrier way to get to know other members of the community. Read more about the WAMM in the next section.

- **They can participate in a Happy Hour.** Few things more consistently bring people together than a happy hour. Every Friday afternoon, Sarah and one or two volunteers get together to mix up some drinks, turn up the music, and turn the kitchen into a hangout spot. In 2013,

Veronica kicked off our weekly happy hours and introduced the idea of passing out shots to everyone at 4:30 p.m. while they're still working, as a way to ensure everyone can participate and also to entice people to stick around when they might have otherwise bolted for the door after wrapping up their work.

Homework: Create a map of all the ways members can connect to each other.

Start by writing down everything you currently do in a stream of consciousness. Then identify any new ideas you may want to add to the mix, using the above list or any new ideas you concoct.

Ideally, you should have a way for people of varying dispositions to connect to the community. It should account for people who identify as introverts and people who identify as extroverts; it should account for people who prefer to socialize during business hours and people who prefer after hours. If there are people in your community who are significantly different in other critical ways, look for how to account for those differences as well.

[5] We hold a monthly Welcome Aboard Member Meeting (WAMM).

On the first Friday of every month from 11:30 a.m. to 12:30 p.m., we hold a simple gathering in our largest conference room and invite a mix of new and longstanding members to gather to get to know each other a little better.

On the Monday before the meeting, Peter and I meet with Sarah to review the list of members we're going to invite.

Who's invited?

- **Any members who have joined since the last meeting.** These folks are the initial group we focus on. In the course of getting these new members registered, Sarah will likely have already informed them of the next meeting, so they should have an expectation already set. While we don't make people attend WAMM, we foster an impression that it's a thing they really ought to do if they want to get the most out of their experience.

- **Any members who have recently joined but haven't attended yet.** Perhaps they missed the previous meeting, or they haven't responded yet to our invitations.

- **Any members who we think might need a boost.** This might be a member who has been around for a while but, for whatever reason, we get the sense that they're needing to re-engage in the community. We want, essentially, to ensure no one slips through the cracks. It's a mistake we've made too many times in the past. Few things hurt like the email you get when someone you had high hopes for quits out of the blue, and only then do you realize you'd done nothing to ensure they were sticking around for long enough that eventually you lost them.

- **Active, well-established members.** At any given time, there are a number of members who are particularly active, comfortable and in the mood to be social. These people are superconductors. They're great. Why not have them in the meeting, too? Sometimes, these people show up to WAMM without us even needing to invite them. (Cherish every one of these people.)

This also gives newcomers a sense that there are fellow members they can turn to if they need to ask a question that they might not feel comfortable asking of the people who run the place. Fostering a sense of permission and safety for members to talk to each other in this way is critical.

- **As many staff members as possible.** Peter, Sarah and I have attended every meeting so far. Leo, our Minister of Fun, has also been to nearly all of the meetings. Since we're now at a scale where we can't quite personally know every member, having this opportunity to at least establish an initial face-to-face interaction gives us a chance to make everyone aware of who we are, why we got into this, and that we're here for them if they need us.

This is handy at deflecting one of the things that inspired dread in me for a long time: the weird feeling of there being someone in the space that I don't quite know if I've ever met before. I hate this feeling. "Have we met? I don't know, I'm sorry, I can't remember." It kills me. WAMM gives me a way to know for sure that we at least met that one time.

How we run a WAMM

1. **I introduce myself.**

   - I thank everyone for coming.
   - I tell people a little bit about myself, the other staff members, and some background on New Work City and why it exists.
   - I explain to them why it's important that we do this meeting.

2. **I then invite everyone to introduce themselves with their:**

   - Name
   - What they're working on
   - How they found us
   - Why they decided to join
   - Anything they could use help with right now
   - What their favorite snack is
     - This is for future use during Snack Wars™, a fun game Leo runs in the space from time to time. Learn more at http://twitter.com/snackwars

3. **We go around in a circle, introducing ourselves.** We allow for some light conversation to emerge from these introductions, as people naturally feel compelled to dive deeper into people's stories and passions.

4. **We look for opportunities to let people know about the tools and resources available to them as a member.** The phrase "post that to the Google Group!" is a mantra that's hard for us to utter too often.

5. **I wrap things up with some reminders.**

   - I remind people that, ultimately, New Work City is the sum total of everyone who's a part of it. I tell them that the culture is something we all shape together. By participating in this gathering, they're now on the other side.
   - I tell them that when someone new sits next to them, they can feel free to introduce themselves.

- I tell them that they can help keep things in order here. Share nicely, and expect nothing less from everyone else. If they see someone stepping out of line, talk to them about it.
- I thank people again.

The WAMM is one of our newer concepts; it arose from a variety of inspirations including a "New Member Cotivation" idea Veronica had been working on for a while, as well as the orientations of other coworking spaces like the Centre for Social Innovation. We put our own spin on it, and so far I think it's been well worth our while.

Homework: Develop an onboarding event of your own

You can use our WAMM as inspiration (reach out to me and let me know how it goes if you do!), or start fresh with your own idea.

[6] We let the members start and stop their own memberships.

We know that our members are people who are going to be moving fluidly throughout the changes in their lives, so we decided our memberships should match. That means a few things:

- **No sign-up or cancellation fees.** One should be able to join or quit without having to pay extra.

- **Cancel anytime.** The only reason we could think of to force someone to give longer notice would be to squeeze more money out of them when they clearly don't want the service anymore. Not our style.

- **Membership starts the day you want to start.** No need to wait for the first of the month, or to prorate the memberships. Membership starts when a member wants to start working, and it stops when you stop paying us. Clean and direct.

- **Upgrade or downgrade anytime.** One can simply cancel their current level and sign up for a new level on the fly.

Because of this fluidity, we have a substantial amount of churn. Membership statuses change on a nearly daily basis. That could mean a lot of work for us if we're not careful. To alleviate that workload while simultaneously reinforcing a sense that one must take responsibility for their membership here, we empowered members to sign up and cancel themselves without nearly any labor required on our end.

I can't tell you that these are the best ways to do business. For all I know, doing things this way has cost us money, but I hated the idea of running a business that charges people for service they don't want. I hoped that we might attract people who would recognize and appreciate that we did business this way, and we have.

If we could start over today, we'd probably use a membership management system like Cobot.me and a more modern, more fully featured and better designed payment platform like Stripe over our current Paypal.

In any case, we'd always reinforce the fact that the power is ultimately in the hands of the individual.

How our DIY membership setup works:

6. **A prospective member first must visit the space.** This gives us a chance to meet them face-to-face and get a basic understanding of who they are and what their expectations are. It also helps us ensure they know what they're getting into. For this, we use ScheduleOnce, which is a highly customizable online booking system. There are many other services that offer something similar; I'd recommend you research all of the options. ScheduleOnce works well for us, but feels just a little more corporate than I'm comfortable with. If you do go with ScheduleOnce, be sure to read the feature sets for the varying membership levels carefully and expect to pay to get more than the minimum level of features so you really have the controls you want.

2. **Once they're ready, we direct them to a custom URL to register.** For this we use Typeform, a system for creating intelligent and nicely designed forms. If you've ever used Google Forms before and have found yourself sick of not being able to make a more attractive and professional looking form, Typeform is your answer. We pay for a level of service that costs $10 per month and it's well worth it.

3. **During the registration process, they are directed to a method of payment.** Where the payment sits in the registration process has been a topic of much discussion, but ultimately we have gone with an approach that ensures no one is able to become a member until they've paid for the privilege. I really wanted to avoid us being ever having to face a situation where a member wasn't a paying member for whatever reason; knowing that everyone in the space has paid to be there alleviates all sorts of potential pressure.1.

As for the method of payment, we use Paypal's subscription service. Since it's no longer 2008 (when we committed to using Paypal as our platform), I'd recommend you use another service. If I were starting a space today, I'd likely use Stripe.

You can, of course, also use an existing membership management platform designed for this purpose. If I were starting from scratch, I'd likely use a platform just for the sake of ease of use and sanity, but keeping memberships portable would be a major requirement. Your mileage may vary.

[7] We make our business hours malleable.

This is an endlessly tricky topic. People have a wide range of desires and needs, and logistical, security and staffing issues abound.

Factors at play

- **Some members want to be able to come in early.** Lots of members want to be able to work late into the evening as well.

- **We can't afford to pay staff to run the place 24/7** with our current business model.

- **If we built a business model around a 24/7 workspace, it would be more complicated to manage,** expose us to greater liability, increase the number of times we get phone calls about problems in the middle of the night, and one other important thing:

- **Explicitly offering around-the-clock access creates opportunities for people to treat their relationship with us as being one that is strictly about access to space.** Space is an extremely valuable resource in central Manhattan, especially on nights and weekends. We are always guarding against exposing ourselves to those who would simply use us for our space. By refusing to formally offer up use of our space 24/7, we dissuade people from wanting to engage with us in a way that is strictly about having that kind of access.

This is part of a general challenge we face when it comes to our identity. We don't want to be perceived as being in the business of renting space, but at the same time our business model is functionally predicated on it. This is no easy thing to balance.

With all of these factors, the intention has always been to forge a way to strike a healthy balance. We want to do a great job of offering a workspace that people can count on as a place they know they can go when they want to really get work done, but we want to gently discourage the notion that we can be used simply as a place to rent space to do work.

There's no clear right answer when it comes to how to make these kinds of calls. We've probably missed out on a lot of potentially good members because we didn't explicitly offer 24/7 access, but we've probably also spared ourselves lots of trouble. I can't say for sure.

What I can say for sure is that we've found some handy ways to unofficially give members lots of much-appreciated flexibility.

Some things we do:

- **We are deliberately vague about our hours.** We say that our staff runs the space from 9 a.m. to 6 p.m., but we don't say that these are our opening and closing hours. The reality is that people are often working in the space long before 9 a.m. and long after 6 p.m.

- **We train people we trust in how to lock up.** Inevitably, there are a handful of members who consistently work late. More often than not, we get to know them quickly. Our system for locking up is pretty straightforward—anyone can do it. Showing someone how to lock up only takes a few minutes. While it could be a little risky to allow people to run the show themselves when we're not around, in six years of running things this way we've never encountered a major issue.

- **We tell newcomers they can work until the last person we've trained to lock up leaves.** In all likelihood, our regulars will work later, so the newcomer should not fear being kicked out. For a lot of people it's extremely valuable to know they need not fear being kicked out right in the middle of a productive streak.

- **We don't formally offer hours past 6 p.m.** We make it clear that we could close up shop at 6 p.m. sharp, but also note that it almost never happens.

- **We make it clear that things work differently here.** We don't close at a strict time, because we trust people to sort it out themselves. It communicates that the line between company and customer is deliberately blurry, because we all make this work together.

- **A small number of trusted members are given keys for early morning access.** This isn't something we offer publicly; no one can come in off the street and expect to be given a key to open up the place. These trusted members are grateful for the access and are generally highly respectful of the unspoken privilege and the responsibility it brings. These members tend to blossom into extremely responsible citizens.

- **We don't offer weekend access to anyone, except as a rare favor.** Coming in early or staying late is one thing; weekends are a different beast altogether. That being said, every once in a while when someone we trust asks us nicely because of some extra-special need, we'll loan them a key.

It would be great if we had a more formal, member-driven system for granting and revoking access to the space on mornings, nights, and weekends. We just haven't gotten it together to implement that kind of structure.

In the meantime, doing things this way has allowed us to offer the hours that members need without having to deal with the complications associated with formally offering those hours.

All it takes is a little bit of trust!

[8] We rely on our culture and our values when we encounter people who we fear may not be a good fit.

Once, we received an inquiry from a guy who fit the perfect profile of someone we didn't want in the space. During his initial tour of the space, he asked questions that made apparent his explicit desire to abuse every one of our shared resources. He gave the distinct impression that he didn't trust us, he didn't expect us to trust him, and he had no intention of having regard for anything other than his own interests.

We had several internal powwows about what to do. Every fiber in every one of us wanted desperately to tell him he wasn't welcome here.

I knew doing so would cross a line we've been adamant about never crossing. We are stewards of a system; it's not our job to decide who stays and who goes. Of course, there does exist a point where we would ask someone to leave. In this guy's case, however, we simply had our intuition to go on. For as much as we all didn't think this guy would be a good fit, we couldn't deny him access for any reason than because of our own vibes. How do you explain that to a guy? That's not our style.

If we let him join, however, what would happen? What if he soured the culture? What if he cost us members with his disruptive behavior?

This, we realized, was a chance for us to prove one of the core hypotheses behind our approach: If our community is the self-curating, self-correcting organism we've designed it to be, then it should be resilient enough to absorb this individual in whatever way it needed to.

I penned carefully worded emails to this person explaining how we worked differently from the highly transactional, dog-eat-dog business relationships he'd clearly grown to expect. I didn't tell him he didn't belong; I didn't tell him not to register. I just stuck to being very clear about what we represent.

He signed up. We took a deep breath.

Do you know what happened? He turned out to be a pretty okay member.

There was some abuse of resources, but we steadfastly held our ground in committing to communicating with him about our values. We took steps to curb bad behavior as much as possible. We kept a close eye on him. When he tested us, we powwowed, we figured out how to approach the situation, and we found a way to focus on educating him on our values.

Before long, he was starting to show signs that he was getting it. He was participating in our discussion group; he was offering help. He wanted to participate. He wanted to share.

He didn't stay for super long, but in the months he was there, I learned a lot about human malleability.

You see, when we say that someone is not a good fit for something, we imply that the person in question is a static entity, impervious to change or persuasion. We assume that the person we see is who they'll always be. The reality is that nothing could be further from the truth.

One of the great joys of running a coworking space has been witnessing how people evolve and blossom and show new sides of themselves over the course of their tenure. For any given new member, but especially for the ones about whom we have concerns, we'd do well to look at who they might be capable of becoming, and not who we perceive them to be.

Part of why we do what we do is to help people un-learn a transactional way of doing business that deserves to fade with the century in which it was born. Helping people learn to do business in a more modern way is something we're all getting the hang of—that's part of the job for us.

I don't know whether we do the greatest job ever at this. I don't know for certain that there are right or wrong answers to these things. But I do know that we've had an open door policy since 2008, and we've never been compelled to abandon it. I know a lot of folks are grateful for it.

New York loves coolness and exclusivity, or at least the illusion of it. We flock to signless speakeasies and line up for Cronuts. It's just a part of this city's culture.

When it comes to coworking, however, openness is such a deeply core part of what we are about. To imply that someone, anyone, might not be good enough to be a part of what we do feels contrary to the spirit of the kind of community we want to have. One's ability to be a part of our community should be in their own hands. By leaving the curation of the community to the community itself, we save ourselves the dubious role of the arbiter and give people who might have no other good option a chance to have a seat at the table.

For those who might not have been accepted into a more exclusive workspace, I take great satisfaction in knowing that we've been able to provide them a haven.

How you do things where you are is up to you. Perhaps you will find something in this story that helps guide you as you consider how to handle difficult calls of your own.

Homework: Determine how to handle people who give you bad vibes

This is a great opportunity for you to work with your team to develop a clear approach to handling not just potentially disruptive folks, but newcomers in general. This can be a document you develop together, or a brainstorming session.

[9] We don't charge extra for printing—or anything else.

When I'm giving a tour, I make a point to wave from one end of the space to another, telling the person that we share everything here. It's important to establish that right away.

As we tour the space, I go one step further when passing our printers. I tell them that we don't charge extra for printing, we just ask that everyone be reasonable. If they need to print a lot, I tell them, they can come talk to us about it or just drop some money in our online Tip Jar. (Our Tip Jar is a simple Paypal button that lets people give us an arbitrary amount of money. This is super handy for all sorts of unpredictable situations.)

I've heard more than a few people talk with disdain about places they've worked at in the past where they were charged for every sheet of paper. It is a practice, literally, of nickel and diming.

It reinforces the idea that we're in the business to sell access to resources, when the reality is that we're in the business of selling access to people. We do anything we can do to avoid reinforcing the cold, transactional nature of simply renting resources.

[10] We let members book our large conference room online.

For our biggest conference room, we use Google Calendar Appointments embedded in a simple web page that includes some other handy information.

How we do it

- **We use a "secret" URL that's technically accessible to anyone, but we only give it out to our part-time and full-time members.** This allows us to minimize the chances that someone will abuse the conference rooms.

- **We let people self-police, but we keep an eye on things.** An email is generated every time someone makes a booking, plus we have the calendar visible at our front desk, so we can easily spot something that seems out of place.

- **We gently inform people of the limitations around usage.** It was only after several years and much consideration that we decided to name and impose a specific limitation on conference room usage (two hours per person per day). In general, we consider rules to be indicative of a failure to foster a healthy culture of trust. When it comes to conference rooms, which are extremely valuable and scarce resources (especially in the middle of Manhattan), we made an exception that has helped us mitigate the effects of this.

Google has messed with its Appointments feature over the years, sometimes trying to deactivate it but still offering it to older accounts, so you may not be able to count on it. For handy alternatives, check out Cobot, ScheduleOnce or Calendly.

[11] We let members book smaller meeting rooms in the space.

We have two mid-sized conference rooms that fit about four people and are used continuously throughout the day.

By using a simple system of paper and whiteboard markers, we're able to give anyone (even a non-member) a way to claim the room in a simple ad-hoc way. No education is required and accessibility is maximized: when you see the system, how it works and your freedom to use it are immediately apparent.

Things we do

- **We post a simple sheet with time slots** to the outside of the room, so people can easily grab an adjacent whiteboard marker and write their name into a time slot.

- **We wipe this board every morning** as part of our opening routine.

Results

- **Accountability.** You have to write your name on the sheet, in pen, where anybody can see. If you're abusing it, it will be obvious not just to us but to anyone walking by.

- **You have to physically be in the space to use it.** This helps us dissuade people from signing up for membership just to abuse our conference rooms.

[12] We offer members a way to help run the place.

Sometimes there are people who really belong in the space, but can't afford full-time membership. The value of having these people in the space is hard to overestimate, so over the years we've developed various ways of giving these people a way to be members without having to pay money for membership. Instead, they pay in the form of some time staffing the front desk.

Veronica, who developed the current version of this, dubbed this the Space Agent program.

How it works:

- **Members work a few shifts per week at the front desk.** The schedule is set in advance and made consistent, so everyone knows who's working when. We train them on the basic things they need to know about maintaining the space and answering common questions.

- **In exchange, each Agent gets a membership** that allows them to work in the space whenever they'd like.

- **We recruit privately.** We're not looking for folks who want to work in our space for free, but folks who would pay to work in our space if they could. You know how Willy Wonka didn't reveal the real reason behind his Golden Ticket contest until the very end? We sometimes do things like that to avoid ulterior motives.

- **We limit the terms and revisit the arrangements periodically.** Historically, any arrangement set in perpetuity is exposed to the relationship degrading over time, so we set finite terms for our relationships with each Space Agent so we have a chance to review how things are going and decide how, or whether, to continue from that point onward.

Doing this helps us in a few critical ways:

- **Newcomers encounter a member first, not an employee.** Immediately, an impression is made that this place isn't just a business whose services are to be consumed. It also gives the newcomer a chance to speak to someone who isn't on payroll, which makes it more likely they'll believe what they hear.

- **Members who belong have a way of being there.** Every member can enrich or detract from the quality of the culture. Inevitably, there are members who are invaluable to the culture of the community who can't afford to be there as often as everyone would love them to be. This gives you a way to get those folks in the door without devaluing what you're offering.

- **We save money on staff.** This is obvious, but not to be overlooked. In our model, we simply can't afford to pay the staff it would take to really manage the front desk well.

When in doubt

Before we bring this journey to a close, let's take a moment to reflect on what it is that we're doing here. A coworking space is, ultimately, the sum total of all of the people who are a part of it—the staff, the members and everyone else whose lives intersect with it throughout the course of its life. While we can so easily get caught up in processes and rules and procedures, so often the best answers come from remembering that ultimately this comes down to human beings who are interacting with each other and building relationships every day.

They're building relationships with each other, with you and with the meta-entity that is your business. Remembering that we're all humans who are in this together can help keep you grounded in a healthy place as you deal with often unpredictable circumstances.

It's weird that we've gotten to a point where so many of us have to deliberately practice treating each other like human beings, but it also means people will appreciate and respond well to it when they see it. Whenever we practice that, things tend to go well for us. When we get caught up in inhuman thinking, things tend not to go so well for us.

If you're being trusting, authentic and real, you invite others to be the same. Practice that every day and you should be well on your way to a happier life, with compatriots by your side who are happy to help clear the sink, refill the coffee pot, connect to each other, manage their memberships, share nicely, and maybe even help you run the place.

Thanks!

Thanks for reading my book! Did anything stand out to you as particularly useful or resonant? Strong or weak? Did these ideas collide with your own in a way that's interesting to you? I'd love to hear from you. Please email me at mugs@nwc.co with your thoughts!

This book is a special thing to me; it draws from many years of experimenting. I hope it's been special to you, too.

If you manage a coworking space or something like it, I believe you have an opportunity to play a role in shifting the world's relationship with work for the better. Redefining work culture in a way that's friendlier and more human is something I'm passionate about; if you're passionate about it too, perhaps together we can make a difference to the people around us and those who are inspired by our stories.

We named our coworking space New Work City in part because we like puns, but also because the analogy of a city is apt. In a city, people gather together in a concentrated place to share resources and opportunity. New Work City is no different but for its scale.

By resolving to come together to share a workspace, we are building little cities of our own that exist, ultimately, for the benefit of every one of its citizens. The more we can bring our work into alignment with that, the better off we'll all be.

Being a part of building a coworking space has been an immensely rewarding experience for me. I hope it is for you, too.

Rock on!